I0169271

THE ALL NEW STYLE OF MAGAZINE-BOOKS

SDM

www.SDMLIVE.com

MP

MOCY PUBLISHING
WWW.MOCYPUBLISHING.COM

Copyright © 2016 SDM Live.
a division of Aye Money Promotions & Publishing, LLC and
Mocy Music Publishing, LLC. All rights reserved.
Printed in the U.S.A.

Printed by CreateSpace, An Amazon.com Company

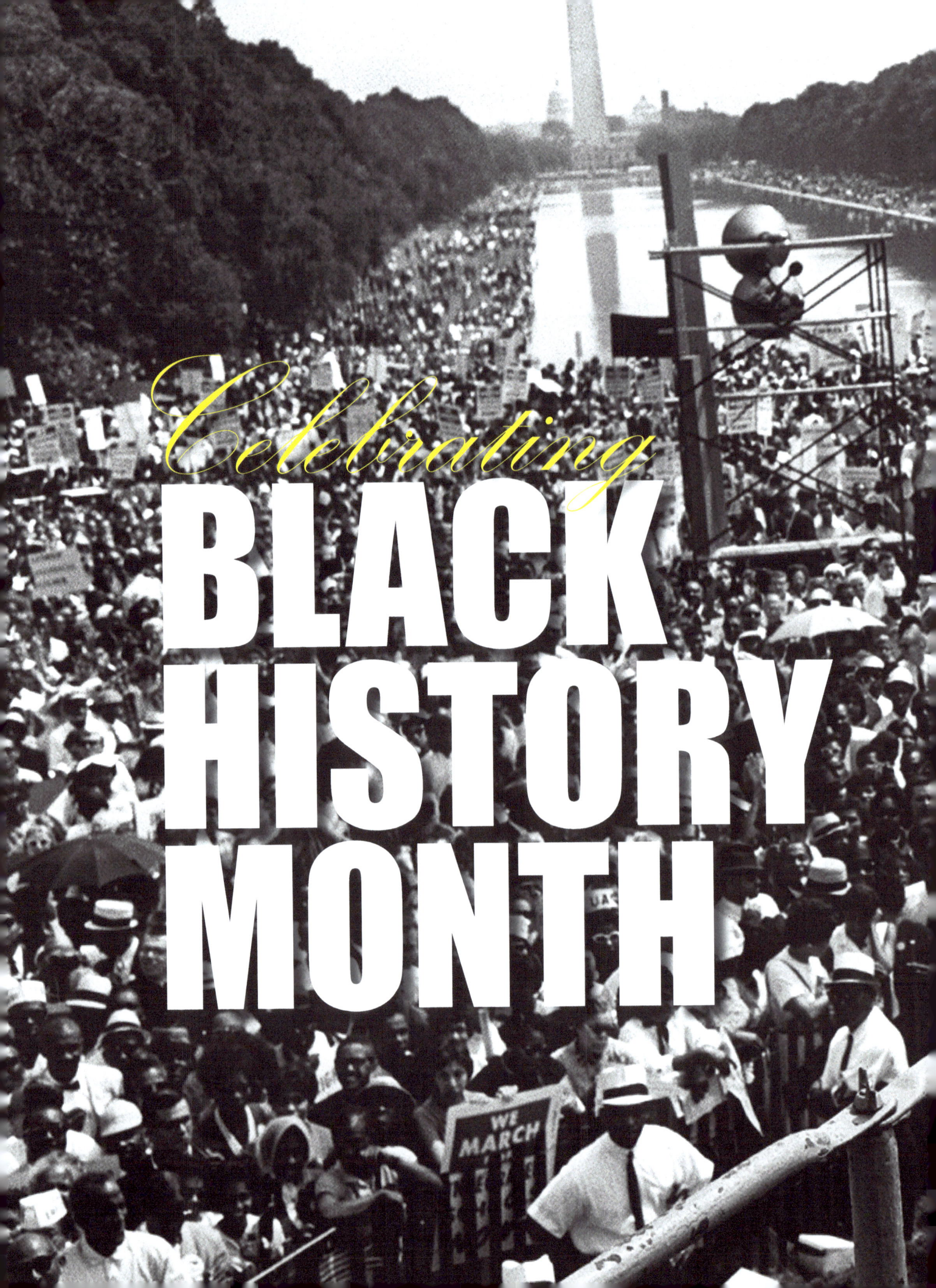

Celebrating

BLACK HISTORY MONTH

SDM

EDITOR-IN-CHIEF
D. "Casino" Bailey
casino@sdmlive.com

EDITORAL DIRECTOR
Sheree Cranford
sheree@sdmlive.com

GRAPHIC/WEB DESIGNER
D. "Casino" Bailey
casino@sdmlive.com

A&R MANAGER
Aye Money
ayemoney@sdmlive.com

ACCOUNT EXECUTIVE
Frank Harvest Jr.
frank@sdmlive.com

PHOTOGRAPHERS
Treagen Colston
D. "Casino" Bailey

CONTRIBUTORS
April Smiley
Courtney Benjamin

COPY ORDERS & ADVERTISING OFFICE
Send Money Order or Check to:
Mocy Publishing
P.O. Box 35195
Detroit, Michigan 48235
(586) 646-8505
advertise@sdmlive.com

Copy Order Item #:
SDM Magazine Issue #2 2015
S&H Plus Retail Price - $9.99 per copy

WWW.SDMLIVE.COM

Printed by CreateSpace, An Amazon.com Company

MP
MOCY PUBLISHING

Copyright © 2016 Support Detroit Movement,
a division of Aye Money Promotions & Publishing, LLC and
Mocy Music Publishing, LLC. All rights reserved.
Printed in the U.S.A.

NO PART OF SDM MAGAZINE, INCLUDING STORIES, ARTWORK, ADVERTISING, OR PHOTO'S MAY BE REPRODUCED BY ANY MEANS WITHOUT THE PRIOR WRITTEN CONSENT FROM MOCY PUBLISHING, LLC. SDM MAGAZINE IS PUBLISHED BY MOCY PUBLISHING, LLC. SDM MAGAZINE WILL NOT ACCEPT ADVERTISING WHICH IS FOUND TO VIOLATE LOCAL, STATE OR FEDERAL LAW.

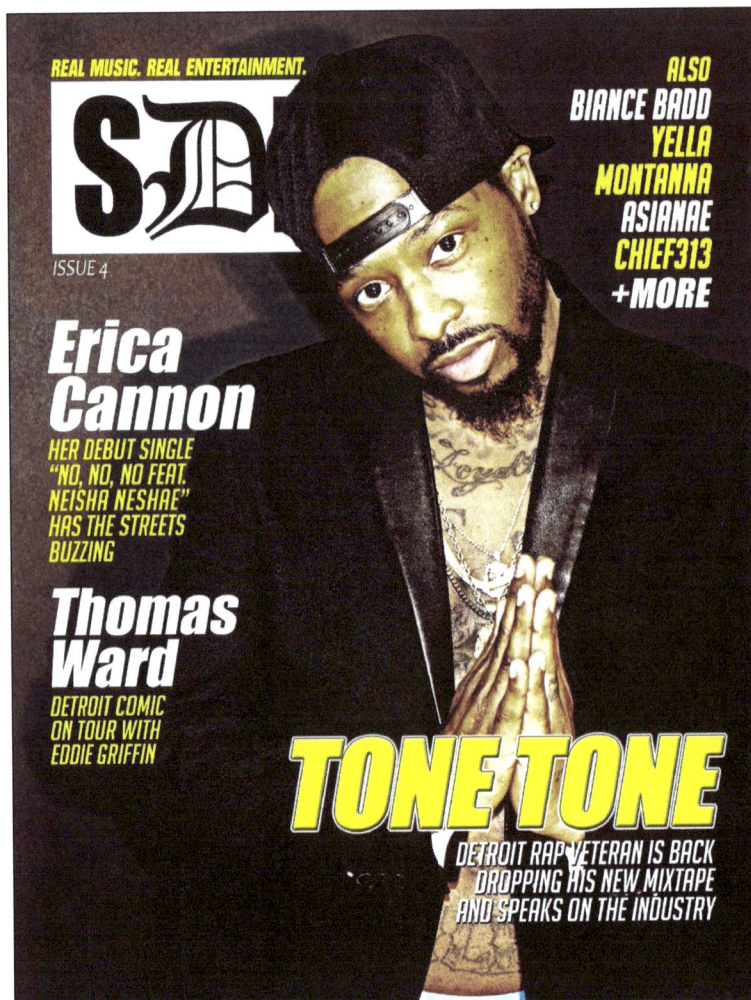

REAL MUSIC. REAL ENTERTAINMENT.
SDM
ISSUE 4

ALSO
BIANCE BADD
YELLA
MONTANNA
ASIANAE
CHIEF313
+MORE

Erica Cannon
HER DEBUT SINGLE "NO, NO, NO FEAT. NEISHA NESHAE" HAS THE STREETS BUZZING

Thomas Ward
DETROIT COMIC ON TOUR WITH EDDIE GRIFFIN

TONE TONE
DETROIT RAP VETERAN IS BACK DROPPING HIS NEW MIXTAPE AND SPEAKS ON THE INDUSTRY

BLACK LIVES MATTER MONTH AVAILABLE IN STORES NOW!!!

Breaking The Generational Curse
By Lamont Williams.

Available from Amazon.com and other online stores

This book is a must read for blacks breaking the curse.

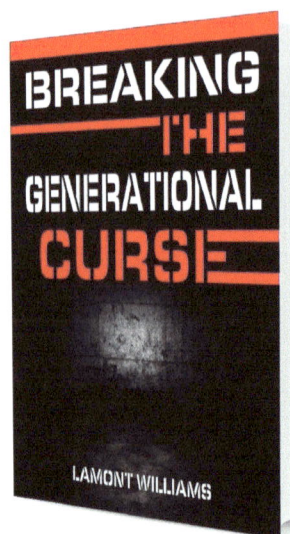

CONTENTS

pg. 12
ERICA CANNON
Her debut single "No, No, No feat. Neisha Neshae" has the streets buzzing.

pg. 16
THOMAS WARD
Detroit Comic on tour with Eddie Griffin.

pg. 20
TONE TONE
Detroit rap veteran is back dropping his new mixtape and speaks on the industry.

pg. 23
TOP 10 CHARTS
The hottest albums and digital singles this month features Rihanna, Tank, Chris Brown, Boosie Badass, and many more.

Techno Show pg. 6

Music News pg. 9

Industry Mix pg. 14

Music Report pg. 19

Top 20 Charts pg. 23

Heels & Skillz pg. 26

Exclusive Cut pg. 29

Next 2 Blow pg. 30

Snap Shots pg. 32

1

Asus - 15.6" Laptop - Intel Core i3 - 4GB Memory - 1TB Hard Drive $299.99
www.bestbuy.com

2

Canon - PIXMA MX922 Network-Ready Wireless All-In-One Printer $87.99
www.canon.com

3

Harman Kardon - Aura Wireless Bluetooth Home Speaker System with Apple AirPlay $314.99
www.harmankardon.com

SweetGhiaccio

The sweet pleasure shop

Call us: 313.757.3848

www.sweetghiaccio.com

sweetghiaccio

www.beatsbydre.com

The Real Timbaland

TIMBALAND'S KING STAYS KING TOUR LANDED AT CLUB BLEU IN DETROIT BUT THE NIGHT ENDED WITHOUT HIM PERFORMING

by Cheraee C.

The legendary producer Timbaland also known as Timbo the King brought his *King Stays King Tour* to Club Bleu in Detroit, Michigan on 1/28/16. He was booked to perform at Club Bleu, but he should've been a no call no show. Timbaland was supposed to be a part of a benefit concert to support Flint and the Flint water crisis. Not only didn't Timbaland perform, but him and his posse were more concerned with getting wasted and being petty. All Timbaland did was drink, drink, take a few pictures for the gram, watch other performers including Neisha Neshae, and drink some more. This is ridiculous because no artist, producer, or celebrity is too good for charity and shouldn't be excessevily drunk at a charity event. If your craft is being a performer/producer and rapping, why wouldn't you perform? A stage is a stage, it wasn't like Timbaland came to Detroit for free.

Overall this wasn't a good look for Timbo. He should've been more of a humanitarian at this event considering he is from the hood as well. Next time he chooses to participate at a charity event, I would advise him to show up and show out completely.

Timbaland

Happiness is a choice

#JustSoYouKnow

The Return of Scarface

STANLEY L. BATTLE WRITES A CLASSIC GANGSTER NOVEL ABOUT THE RETURN OF A CRIMINAL ICON AND HIS EMPIRE.

by Cheraee C.

Have you ever thought about their being a continuation to the 1993 Thriller Scarface? Mocy Publishing presents "The Son of Scarface" - Part 1 which is the literary sequel to the movie Scarface. This book is phenomenal and well-detailed as the author captures every experience, memory, and scene with conviction. The author uses a symbolic language that is hip and original. Most importantly, this book takes place in Detroit. If you are into books that feature heavy content with every type of drug you can imagine, the most violent scenes, mobster affliations, and conniving ways, The Son of Scarface - Part 1 is definitely a book you should add to your gangster library.

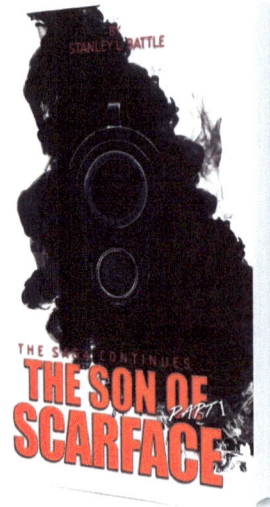

The Son of Scarface Part 1
By Stanley L. Battle

Available from Amazon.com and other online stores

EXPERIENCE. ENJOY. THE AUTHOR.

CHERAEE C.

ph: (734) 752-8253

email: sosyree@cheraeec.com

Intellectual I Hood I Reality Fiction

Books Available at:
Amazon, Kindle, Cheraeec.com and Mocypublishing.com

LET'S GET THAT BOOK PUBLISHED!

RELEASING AN INDEPENDENT RECORD

6th EDITION

by Gary Hustwit

~Where Dreams Become Reality...

AS LOW AS $399.99

* COVER DESIGN
* EDIT BOOK
* PROOF BOOK
* PUBLISH BOOK
* PROMOTE BOOK

Sell your book on Amazon, Kindle Barnes & Noble, and over 1000 bookstores.

WWW.MOCYPUBLISHING.COM

Erica Cannon: Detroit Royalty

DETROIT'S OWN ERICA CANNON IS ON HER WAY TO BLOWING UP
THE POP AND R&B SENSATION IS TOPPING CHARTS WITH HER SINGLE

by Cheraee C.

Q. What is your role in the music industry?

A. I'm an upcoming R&B and pop singer from Detroit currently known for my single "No, No, No featuring Lil George and Neisha Neshae."

Q. Describe how you feel about being a woman that's breaking into the music industry.

A. Being a woman breaking into the music industry is a job that you almost have to be perfect to accomplish. I guess you can say it's a bittersweet feeling and that I am blessed with this opportunity.

Q. Describe your view of other women in the Detroit music business.

A. I view the women of Detroit music as natural born leaders with the ambition to make there mark on the world with their words and their grind.

Q. Describe how it felt to be a part of the Street Hitta Dj's movement and be a part of a lineup with some Detroit heavy hitters including Icewear Vezzo and Neisha Neshae.

A. To be a part of the Street Hitta Dj's movement was an overwhelming feeling that still hasn't hit me. The fact that I have only been doing music altogether for eight months and to receive that call lets me know that I'm on the right path and to go harder. I really appreciate the love.

Q. If you could collaborate with any mainstream artist who would you collab with and why?

A. If I could collaborate with any mainstream artist it would have to be Nicki Minaj. I feel like we would cook up a hit since we are both hip-hop/pop artists and I know the boys would love it.

Biance Badd Talks Work

A DIVA OF R&B, A VIDEO VIXEN, AND A MODEL, BIANCE BADD IS NO STRANGER TO HARD WORK IN THE INDUSTRY .

by Cheraee C.

Q. What is your role in the entertainment industry?
A. I am a singer, songwriter, video vixen, model, promoter, and host at the Bullfrog. My role in the entertainment industry is to simply entertain. To make a connection with the audience and give everything I was blessed with back out to the universe so that they can bless someone else.

Q. Describe your experience being in M City Jr's video Addicted to my Ex.
A. I was beyond blessed to play the lead role in M city Jr's hit record "Addicted to me Ex." I learned a lot being on set and I was able to work with a lot of extremely talented people. The experience was amazing; I was able to work on a little of my acting skills and as you all can see I lived my part lol.

Q. What other Detroit artists' videos have you been in?
A. I've been in Trick Trick video "Outlaw" and a few upcoming Detroit artists one including Dame.

Q. Do you feel like artists can be successful in Detroit or its better to move to another city to pursue music success?
A. I do believe that you can become successful in Detroit, but to have longevity in music you must venture off to other cities and states to get a higher level of success. I feel as if you can be successful pursuing music anywhere as long as you believe in yourself and believe in God.

Q. Describe your experience watching artists perform at the Bullfrog.
A. To be honest I can't believe how much talent the city of Detroit really has to offer! I've watched artists perform for the first time in their life and much more experienced artists, but what they all have in common is drive and determination! I've watched some artists become super stars after weeks and weeks of performing. It's an amazing experience to hear the new music and talent before it hits the streets.

Q. Describe your view of Detroit artists do you think they all sound the same.
A. I think most Detroit rappers do sound the same but it's quite a few that's original and have their on sound. As far as females artists in Detroit we all bring something different to the table and we don't try to sound alike.

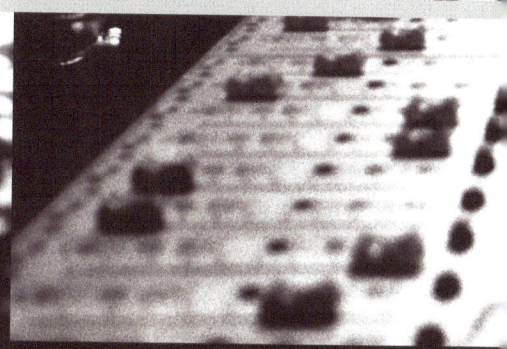

ASPIRE
THE BUSINESS OF BUSINESS

* List Your Compa[ny]
* Attract More Cus[tomers]
* Refer Other Mem[bers]
* Earn 70% Comm[ission]

Become a member and sa[ve]
50% on products and servi[ces]
other members in the netw[ork]

Also earn cash by signing [up]
other members. We offer o[ur]
affiliates the highest earnin[g]
up to 85% commission on [each]
membership referral.

LIST YOUR BUSINESS FOR FREE LIMITED TIME OFFER!

[DIR]ECTORY

THE BEST
BUSINESS D[IRECTORY]
IN THE WORL[D]

[...]biz2biz.com

visit us: www.as[pire...]

Bringing Fun Back to Comedy

THOMAS WARD IS A COMICAL VETERAN WITH A NEW MOVIE UNDERWAY TITLED "ONCE UPON A TIME IN DETROIT."

by Cheraee C.

Q: What is your role in the entertainment industry?
A: A filmmaker and a down-to-earth comic who's been doing comedy for twenty-three years. During a peak of self-development and growth where I experienced being unmarketable as a comic, some health issues, marriage, divorce, and parenthood who would have ever thought Eddie Griffin would've reached out to me.

Q: How do you feel about comedy today?
A: New comics suck; they are arrogant, rude, and do not show homage to legendary comics who established the art of comedy such as Redd Foxx or Richard Pryor. New comics think they are already famous because of their social media stats, but social media don't make a comic good.

Q: How does it feel to be on tour with Eddie Griffin?
A: It's an amazing and incredible experience. Eddie Griffin is the best comedian in the world and being on tour with someone of his stature is a good feeling and a part of being successful.

Q: If you could be on tour with any other comic other than Eddie Griffin who would it be?
A: Other comics would be too worried to be on tour with me because I'm too funny, but at the end of the day money talks. I really can't see myself being on tour with a comedian other than Eddie Griffin.

Q: Tell us something interesting about you.
A: Working on a film that will be releasing soon titled "Once Upon a Time in Detroit." It

is produced by Joe Blount, starring Rodney Perry and Arlen "Griff" Griffin, and was filmed in Detroit, MI.

Q: How can people find you on social media?
A: Facebook @Thomas Ward Twitter @badtweettward

MailCall

This new website hopes to bridge the gap between criminals behind bars and the outside world.

PrisonerMailCall.com lists photos and contact information of inmates looking to share intimate letters with just the right stranger.

The site says that many prisoners are 'fun' and 'loving' like everyone else... but they've just committed felonies.

GET A LISTING FOR 90 DAYS FOR ONLY A $1.00

Search MALE AND FEMALE INMATES Today!!!

www.PrisonerMailCall.com

Tidal Leaks Rihanna

OOPS!!! TIDAL LEAKS RIHANNA'S NEW ALBUM BEFORE RELEASE.

by Semaja Turner

One Michigan city that has the world's full attention is Flint and it's current water crisis.. Back in April 2014, residents claimed the Flint River was contaminated. Now most recently there has been lead contamination cases reported, a polluted water system, and all types of infectious outbreaks. Since the governor Rick Synder didn't resolve the water crisis, President Obama stepped in and declared a federal state emergency for Flint which will give them $5 million dollars in federal aid.

Celebrities from all over the world are campaigning, throwing fundraisers, donating money, donating food, clothing, water purifiers, and donating cases of water to the families of Flint. P.Diddy, Mark Walhberg, Big Sean, Kem, Aretha Franklin, Meek Mill, Madonna, and many more are giving back to the Flint community. Celebrities are even challenging other celebrities to top their charities and donations.

Even though, this is a crisis, its good to see how Americans are truly kind-hearted humanitarians and unite when a national disaster strikes.

The Return of Tone Tone

TONE TONE HAS BEEN REPPING FOR DETROIT MUSIC FOR OVER A DECADE AND IS STILL KILLING THE MUSIC GAME

by Cheraee C.

Q. Describe how long you've been in the music industry and how you have evolved as an artist?

A. I've been in the music industry for about 10 or 11 years. I just never stopped recording and got better and better. Practice makes perfect you feel me.

Q. Describe your experience being signed to Jazze Pha's record label Sho'nuff Records.

A. Being signed with Jazze opened up doors for me, but then again it put a lot of pressure on me because people are always wondering what's next and when you waiting on labels to make a move it can be forever and the hype dies down.

Q. Describe how you feel about Detroit music today since you came on the scene and being an independent artist?

A. It's cool errbody just trying to make it from my point of view #yadigg. I love being an independent artist; I do what da hell I want when I want.

Q. Do you feel like record labels take away from artists as individuals?

A. Yes record labels ain't shit. They watch you do all the hardwork and once you catch a wave they jump on the bandwagon #DBF #FGM #GOLDGANG.

Q. Describe who were some of the best artists you worked with thus far and why?

A. TLC, Twista, Trina, B.G. free bro, my nigga Llyod dope as hell, Gucci Mane who's on my new single "Gold Rolex," and I can't forget being in the studio with Too Short was the shit.

Q. What can we expect from you in 2016?

A. You can expect a lot from me. My new mixtape *11627* hosted by DJ Drama will be dropping 3/3/16 and my current single "Gold Rolex featuring Gucci Mane" is out.

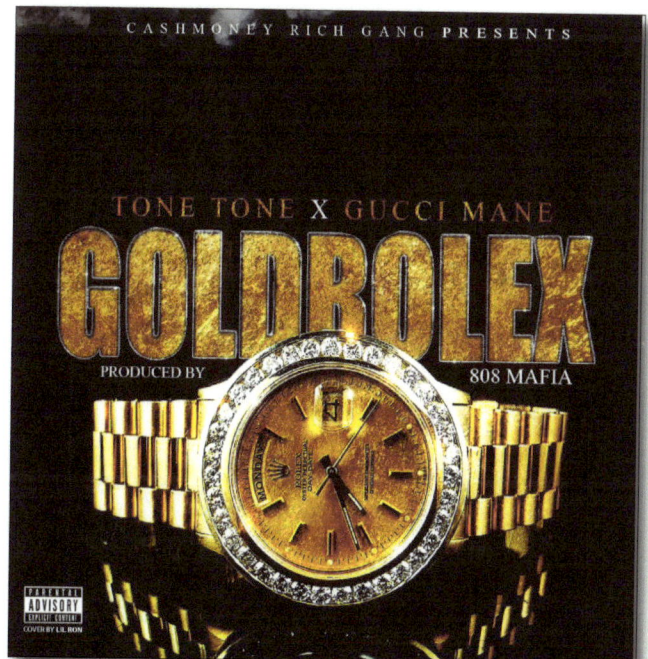

REAL MUSIC. REAL ENTERTAINMENT.

S.D.M

ISSUE 3

ALSO
AUHMAZ!N
ISHMAELSOUL
MZ. PLATINUM
KID JAY

KOSTA
JUST HIT THE JACKPOT WITH A NEW SMASH HIT SINGLE "LOTTERY"

BIGG DAWG BLAST
LAUNCHES THE STREET HITTA DJ'S MOVEMENT

Neisha Neshae

BRINGING IN 2016 ON STAGE WITH THE KING OF R&B R-KELLY & DROPPING A NEW MIXTAPE

PLUS MORE

THE RED CARPET EDITION
SUPERSTARS CAME WITH FASHION AT THE SDM MAGAZINE RELEASE PARTY

US - $9.99   CANADA - $14.99

0 1 >

9 770317 847001

JANUARY 2016 No.3
WWW.SDMLIVE.COM

ORDER YOUR ISSUE FOR $9.99
Send money order plus $3.95 S&H to: Mocy Publishing, LLC
P.O. 35195 * Detroit, MI 48235

TOP 10 CHARTS

TOP 10 DIGITAL SINGLES AND ALBUMS
FEBRUARY 1, 2016

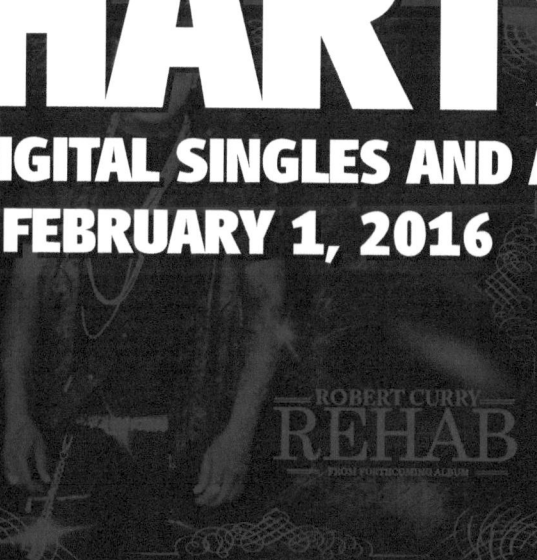

TOP 10 CHARTS

REE-REE PERFORMS HER NEW SINGLE "WORK FT. DRAKE."

TOP #1

Rihanna
Work ft. Drake

*Coming in at #1 this month, **Rihanna** drops a new twerkin track featuring Drake"Work".*

TOP 10 SINGLES
CHART OF THE MONTH

No.	Artist - Song Title
1	RIHANNA - WORK FT. DRAKE
2	TYRESE - SHAME
3	JEREMIH - OUI
4	KENDRICK LAMAR - ALRIGHT
5	KANYE WEST - REAL FRIENDS
6	NEISHA NESHAE - ON A CLOUD
7	YUNG THUG - BEST FRIEND
8	DRAKE - HOTLINE BLING
9	LYNN CARTER - TOO LITTLE
10	RICH MOOK - YES I DO

TOP 10 ALBUMS
CHART OF THE MONTH

No.	Artist - Album Title
1	CHRIS BROWN - ROYALTY
2	TYRESE - BLACK ROSE
3	TANK - SEX, LOVE & PAIN II
4	JANET - UNBREAKABLE
5	DRAKE & FUTURE - WHAT A TIME TO BE ALIVE
6	AYE MONEY - SDM COMPILATION (VOLUME 2)
7	BOOSIE BADASS - IN MY FEELINS
8	THE GAME - THE DOCUMENTARY 2
9	J. COLE - 2014 FOREST HILLS DRIVE
10	DRAKE - IF YOU'RE READING THIS IT'S TOO LATE

NIKE ®

JUST DO IT.

ALBUM REVIEW

Royalty

ARTIST: Chris Brown
REVIEWER: Casino B.
RATING: 4

Mr. Chris Brown releases another masterpiece "Royalty." With an album cover featuring his beautiful daughter, Chris looks like he's at peace and in a new world. The album starts off with the smash hit "Back to Sleep" which describes how he lays it down in the bed with the ladies. Chris also drops another hit single with the track "Liquor."

Chris has recovered pretty while from his past life and is on the mission to conquer the world. This album is a true reflection of who he is now. I rated it a banger.

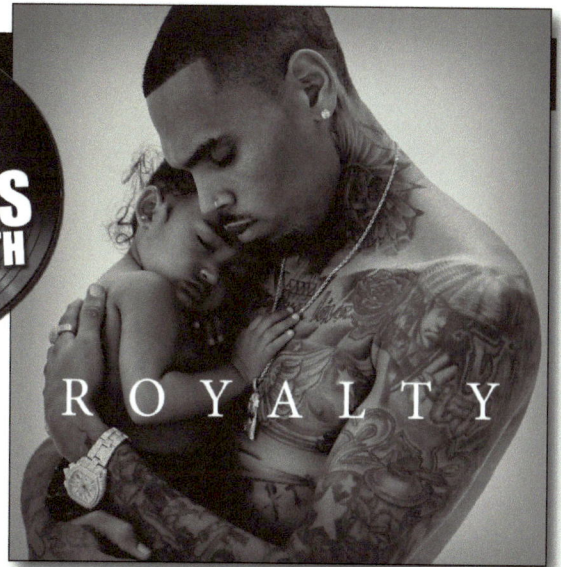

BLACK LIVES MATTER
www.BlackLivesMatter.com

RATE METER: 1 - WACK   2 - NEEDS WORK   3 - STRAIGHT   4 - BANGER   5 - CLASSIC

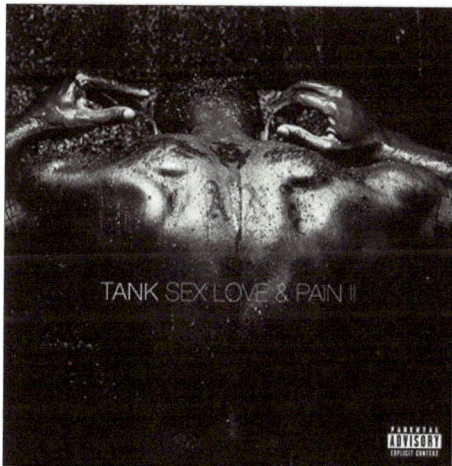

Sex, Love & Pain II

ARTIST: Tank
REVIEWER: Cheraee C.
RATING: 4

Tank has just released the part 2 to his 2007 album Sex, Love, and Pain giving us another round of more sex, more love, and more pain. As always he uses his smooth R&B sound and lyrics to keep it trill with his fans. His LP features appearances by Rich Home Quan, Yo Gotti, Wale, Chris Brown, Sage the Gemini, and more. I give his album four stars.

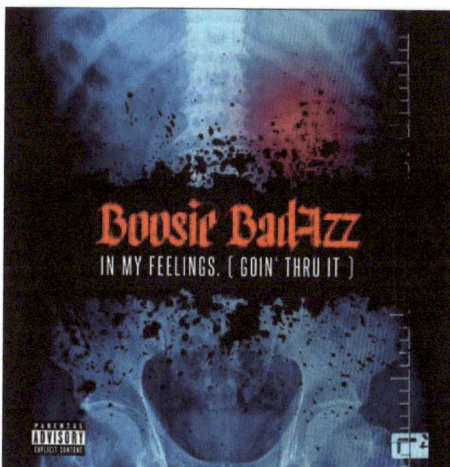

In My Feelings

ARTIST: Boosie Badass
REVIEWER: Cheraee C.
RATING: 4

Much like the album title "In My Feelings" Boosie is in his feelings about the most recent events that has transpired in his life. He wanted to give his fans a personal look into his battle with cancer and rap about how he felt about life and death during that period. The real gets even realer, I give his album four stars.

 MUSIC

HEELS & SKILLZ

MICAH
is am a full-time model
from Detroit, MI,
a part-time personal
assistant, and an
aspiring singer.

instagram
IG @tiana_1211
FB @Micah Taylor

Photography by
@Terance Drake

HEELS &
SKILLZ

Yella Montanna
is a dancer, model,
video vixen, designer,
and a party host.

instagram
@_yellamontanna

Photography by
T-Rich Films

Conciousness
is a beautiful model
for barearmy.

Photography by
@treagenkier

FREE BIRTHDAY PARTIES

EVERY SUNDAY
JAMAICAN
ME KRAZY
The Return
ON STEROIDS

NIKI'S NIGHTLIFE
735 BEAUBIEN ST. | DETROIT, MI

HOSTED BY CHUCKY IV
8 PM - 2 AM | COVER $10 | LADIES FREE TIL 11 PM
$3 DRINK SPECIALS UNTIL 11PM
facebook: CARIBBEAN CONNECTION PROMOTIONS
313.964.1400 | 248.885.2617

SPONSORED BY: CÎROC

BLACK LIVES MATTER
www.BlackLivesMatter.com

Bad Flint H20

FLINT'S WATER CRISIS HAS THE WHITE HOUSE'S ATTENTION AND IS BEYOND MICHIGAN POLITICS.

by Semaja Turner

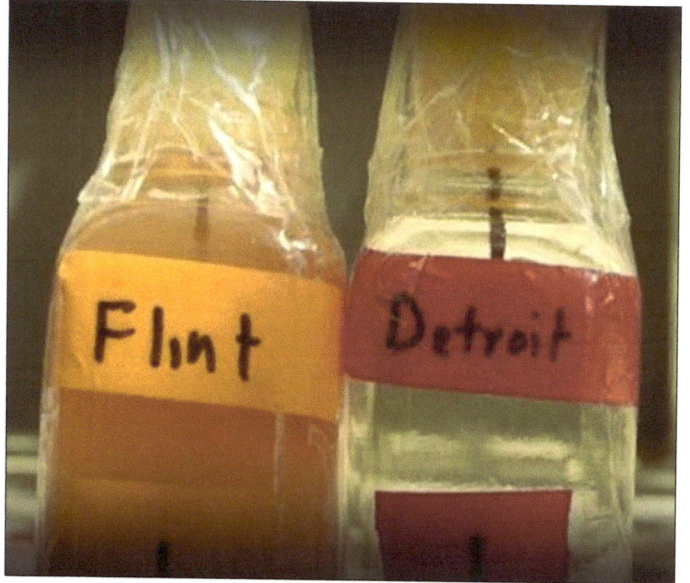

One Michigan city that has the world's full attention is Flint and it's current water crisis.. Back in April 2014, residents claimed the Flint River was contaminated. Now most recently there has been lead contamination cases reported, a polluted water system, and all types of infectious outbreaks. Since the governor Rick Synder didn't resolve the water crisis, President Obama stepped in and declared a federal state emergency for Flint which will give them $5 million dollars in federal aid.

Celebrities from all over the world are campaigning, throwing fundraisers, donating money, donating food, clothing, water purifiers, and donating cases of water to the families of Flint. P.Diddy, Mark Walhberg, Big Sean, Kem, Aretha Franklin, Meek Mill, Madonna, and many more are giving back to the Flint community. Celebrities are even challenging other celebrities to top their charities and donations.

Even though, this is a crisis, its good to see how Americans are truly kind-hearted humanitarians and unite when a national disaster strikes.

NEXT 2 BLOW

SHAKIA SNOW

Q. What is your current position in the music industry?
A. I'm a FEMCEE and I've been pushing my music for a while now. I'm mostly known for having bars; the pit-bull in a skirt feel me. My mixtape is due to drop May/June and it's titled "Young Jada."

Q. How do you feel about female artists in the music industry today and what sets you apart from other femcees?
A. I feel like the artists today are representing themselves and Hip Hop culture with what makes them feel good. I feel like as female emcees we all are united. We all got something to say- feel me, but I can only speak for me. I just know I spit from my heart and I hope the streets love it #100.

Q. Out of all the Detroit artists' you've worked with thus far, what artist did you enjoy working with the most and why?
A. I've worked with so many known Detroit artists, but I will name Bizarre from D12. It was a blessing to work with them and a beautiful experience. I've done St. Andrews with Bizarre and I'm featured on "Return of the Dozen Vol.2." I have two songs with Bizarre called "Cypher" and "14 Emcees."

Q. As an artist do you think it's more important to be mainstream or to make music?
A. As an artist I think it's more important for you to just make music and push yo products to the people. Put out quality and the mainstream will come along as you got something the people want to hear.

Q. If you could collab with a mainstream artist who would you collaborate with and why?
A. If I could collab with a mainstream artist I would collab with Sade because she makes timeless music.

Photography by
@A List Photography

Q. How long have you been doing music and do you plan to get a record deal or stay independent and do music?

A. I've been doing music all of my life, but I got serious about it seven years ago when I was thirteen. I plan on getting a record deal and being a national and international artist.

Q. Describe what sets you apart from other women in your genre.

A. I write and sing what I feel. Everything I've written is a song about what I've actually went through. I get very personal with my performances and I make sure people feel like they know me as a person and an artist before I leave the stage.

Q. How do you feel about women in Detroit music today?

A. I feel like every woman in Detroit music worked like a slave to get where they are because it's not easy coming out of this city. I respect them, but they are my competition before anything else.

Q. Describe your experience being a woman and being in the music industry.

A. Being a woman in the music industry is great, but challenging at times because I'm approached, but I have to let people know I'm about my business and my music, but at the same time I have to be nice about it so no bridges are burned.

Q. What Detroit artists have you worked with?

A. I've done features for many different artists in Detroit, but I've done a few collabs with B. Ryan and King Lynxx.

Q. If you could collab with a mainstream artist who would you collab with and why?

A. If I could collab with a mainstream artist it would be Chris Brown because I feel like his voice extremely advanced

Asianae

and I would have fun while at the same time making good music and hit records.

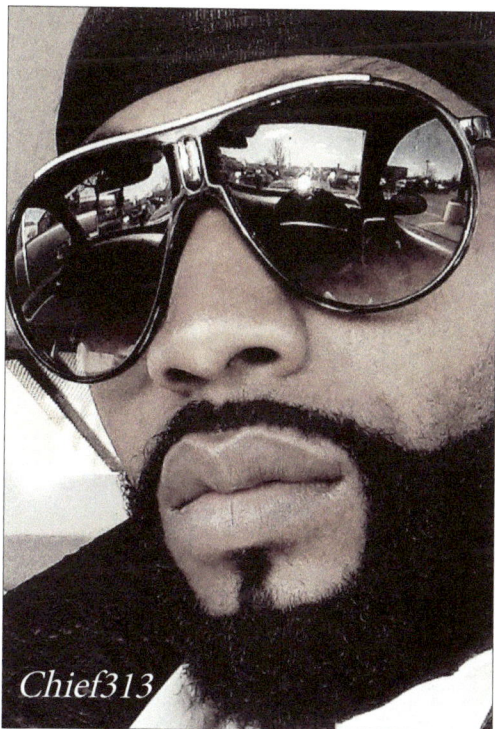

Q. Describe your role in the music industry and what's your story? The main story you trying to get across to the world?

A. My role is being a leader starting a new empire. The main story is on how you can make a change within yourself and become a leader.

Q. You mentioned you're trying to start an empire, so what is your empire and what does your empire entail?

A. My empire is CHIEF ENT and my label will open doors for other upcoming artists. I produce, I make my own tracks, record my own songs, mix and master my own album covers etc.

Q. Describe the inspiration behind why you rap and your lyrics.

A. I get to tell the world my story on my lifestyle pure from the heart how

the system operates. I came from a family of six. I was born in St. Louis and raised in Detroit living from shelter to shelter. I grew up without a father so I decided to take all my anger out in music and create something positive.

Q. Describe your view of Detroit rappers and do you feel like there is an empire out here like the one you are trying to build?

A. Everybody have skills, not everybody, but we need to stick together. It's a lot of hitters in Detroit. Different strokes for different folks, but not like mines. I have so much in stall I just need that right boost.

Q. What can we expect from you in 2016?

A. Videos, movies, events, and more.

Chief313

SNAP SHOTS

Email Your Snap Shots to
snapshots@sdmlive.com

PHARRELL WILLIAMS

adidas®

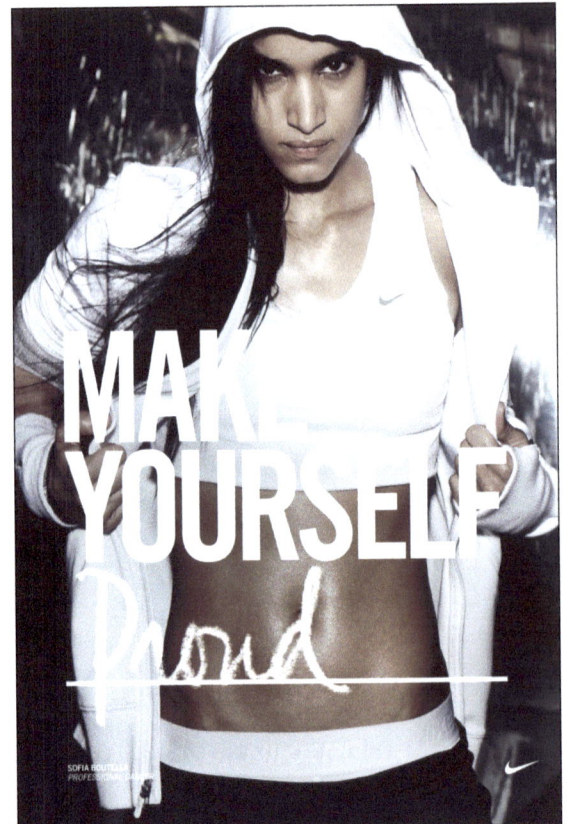

WE HAVE THE LOWEST PRINTING PRICES IN THE NATION

250 EVENT TICKETS
FULL-COLOR ON BOTH SIDES ON THICK UV COATED 14 PT

only $45

1000 BUSINESS CARDS
FULL-COLOR ON BOTH SIDES ON THICK UV COATED 14 PT

only $25

1000 4X6 CLUB FLYERS
FULL-COLOR ON BOTH SIDES ON THICK UV COATED 14 PT

only $65

Need a Design? Add $20 for Business Card or $40 for Flyer

2x5ft VINYL BANNER
FULL-COLOR IN or OUTDOOR BANNER w/GROMMETS

only $99

5000 BUSINESS CARDS
FULL-COLOR ON BOTH SIDES ON THICK UV COATED 14 PT

only $99

2500 4X6 CLUB FLYERS
FULL-COLOR ON BOTH SIDES ON THICK UV COATED 14 PT

only $85

CHECK OUT MORE SPECIALS & ORDER ONLINE ANYTIME: WWW.5DSPRODUCTIONS.COM

1.888.718.2999

5DS PRODUCTIONS®
THE PRINT MEDIA CENTER.

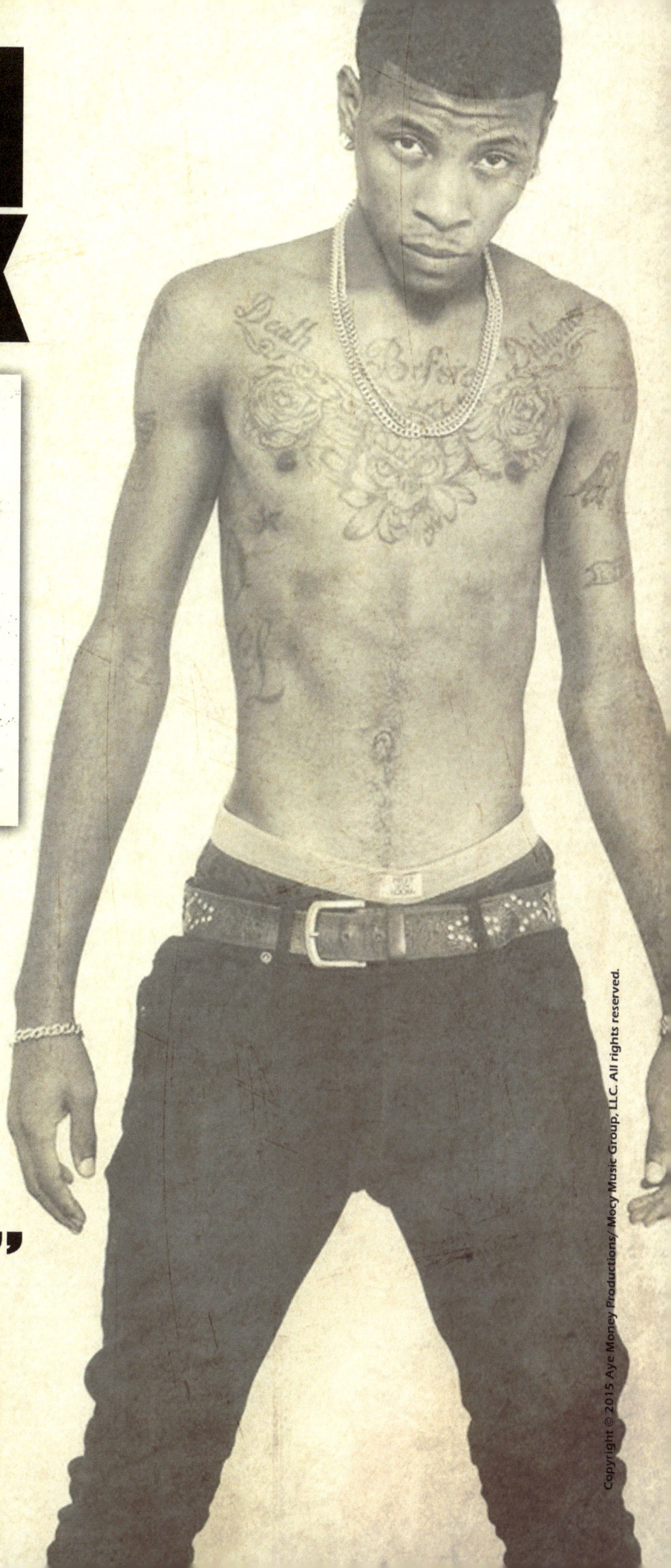

THE ALL NEW STYLE OF MAGAZINE-BOOKS

For advertisement
please call (586) 646-8505
or visit www.sdmlive.com